D1713392

A Great Admiration

A Great Admiration

H.D./Robert Duncan

Correspondence 1950–1961

Edited by Robert J. Bertholf

The Lapis Press

nice 1992

The Lapis Press
589 N. Venice Blvd.
Venice CA 90291

Book design and production by Les Ferriss
Set in Janson by Ann Flanagan Typography
Printed in the United States of America

Library of Congress Cataloging-in-Publication Data

H. D. (Hilda Doolittle), 1886–1961.
   A great admiration : H. D. / Robert Duncan correspondence,
   1950–1961 / edited by Robert J. Bertholf.
      p.   cm.
   Includes bibliographical references.
      ISBN 0-932499-34-1 : $20.00
      1. H. D. (Hilda Doolittle), 1886–1961—Correspondence.
2. Duncan, Robert Edward, 1919–1988—Correspondence.
3. Poets, American—20th Century—Correspondence.
I. Duncan, Robert Edward, 1919–1988. II. Bertholf, Robert J.
III. Title.
PS3507.O726Z485   1992
811'.52—dc20
[B]   92-16850
                                              CIP

Acknowledgments

The originals of the letters of H.D. to Robert Duncan, the originals of the letters of Robert Duncan to H.D., and the original letter of Robert Duncan to Norman Holmes Pearson are now housed in the Beinecke Rare Book and Manuscript Library of Yale University, and are published here with the library's permission. One letter of Duncan to H.D., dated 11 September 1960, is housed with the Robert Duncan Collection in The Poetry / Rare Books Collection, The University at Buffalo, State University of New York, and is published here with the library's permission. Permission to publish the letters of H.D. to Robert Duncan has been granted by Perdita Schaffner for The Estate of Hilda Doolittle; and permission to publish the letters of Robert Duncan to H.D. has been granted by the Literary Estate of Robert Duncan. The photographs of Robert Duncan and Jess are from the Robert Duncan Collection and are reproduced here with the permission of The Poetry / Rare Books Collection, the University at Buffalo, State University of New York, and the Literary Estate of Robert Duncan. The photograph of H.D. is from the Beinecke Rare Book and Manuscript Library of Yale University, and is reproduced here with the library's permission. I wish to acknowledge the assistance of John Michael Boughn, Michael Basinski, Marta Werner, the staff of The Poetry / Rare Books Collection and Les Ferriss of The Lapis Press in the preparation of the text.

Editor's Introduction

"The War Trilogy," Robert Duncan wrote to H. D. on 20 July 1959, "made it possible, gave link in a tradition, for me to follow lines of my inheritance within the main body of a given poetics." In the first chapter of "The H. D. Book," Duncan recounts the story of Miss Keough teaching H. D.'s poem "Heat" in a high school English class in Bakersfield, California. From the beginning of his life as a writer, H. D. was an immediate presence. Duncan found great satisfaction in drawing out his lines of derivation as poet. He read the modernist writers of the first part of the twentieth century, and so Ezra Pound, William Carlos Williams, James Joyce, Wyndham Lewis, Gertrude Stein, W.B. Yeats, Virginia Woolf, D. H. Lawrence, and others began appearing in his notebooks and essays. "It was not until *The Walls Do Not Fall*," Duncan writes, "that H. D. would take her place, along with Ezra Pound and Williams, as master for me in my Art."

By 1944, when *The Walls Do Not Fall* appeared in book form, Duncan had lived in New York City, and knew the artists and writers surrounding Anais Nin. He edited a magazine, *Retort*, established connections with James Peter Cooney, whose magazine *The Phoenix* supplied further connections with literary anarchists; he had been in and out of the army, and in and out of a marriage. He had published a poem in *Poetry*. In 1945 he returned to California and began the literary life that led to the publication of his first major book, *The Opening of the Field* in 1960. After 1945, H. D.'s poetry and prose provided a decisive link with the modernist tradition which began in Imagism before World War I and culminated in "The War Trilogy," The *Pisan Cantos* and *Paterson* after World War II. As the correspondence shows, the connection with Freud, the realm of mystery, as well as the poetry, charged Duncan's devotion to H.D.'s writing. The metaphors of "thread" and "tapestry" that inform "The H.D. Book," mainly the discussions of "The War Trilogy," also appear in the letters. From May 1960 until H.D.'s death, Duncan focused on her work to mark his link to a literary tradition at the same time that he was writing to her and sending her his new poems. He was living out the actual thread that linked his writing to a tradition.

Duncan wrote to his masters in poetry, and when possible, made trips to see them. In 1943 he visited Laura Riding in Florida, in August 1947 he visited Ezra Pound in St. Elizabeth's in Washington, D.C., and in May 1960 he visited H.D. in New York City. That visit centers this correspondence. In April of the same year Duncan gave a reading at Yale University, where Norman Holmes Pearson was his host. Pearson commissioned Duncan to write an homage for H.D.; on 3 May 1960, before meeting H.D., Duncan wrote to him: "My mind returns whenever it can to the matter, and with the notes I have I have some hope that early in June I will be prepared to send you a sketch of the book and we can make our arrangements for me to set to work." By 27 May, after meeting H.D., Duncan wrote "I set about the H.D. Book." With the letter dated 1 and 12 October 1960, Duncan sent a 16 page typescript, which became, after the revisions of 1964, the first chapter of the first part of "The H.D. Book." The book was intended as an homage for H.D.'s birthday. At this point there was no indication that the book would turn into a major discussion of modernist poetics that intensified and formulated Duncan's life as a poet.

The correspondence demonstrates Duncan realizing, again, his commitment to H.D.'s writing, and to his own poetry derived from that commitment. Two poems grow out of this correspondence, "A Sequence of Poems for H.D's Birthday" and "After Reading H.D.'s *Hermetic Definitions*." The first is a tribute to H.D., and was finished a few days after her birthday, 10 September 1959. The second poem, however, has caused a little controversy. Duncan wrote to H.D. on 7 April 1961 that "Hermetic Definitions" arrived safely. From the beginning Duncan spelled "Definitions" as plural and not as singular, as H.D. had written in her text. When Duncan published his poem "After Reading H.D.'s *Hermetic Definitions*" [*Trobar* (1962)], eager readers wanted access to H.D.'s unpublished poem. Copies circulated, but until Harvey Brown's edition of *Hermetic Definition* (West Newbury, MA: Frontier Press, 1971) provoked the printing of an authorized text (New York: New Directions, 1972) the poem was not available to the reading public. Duncan maintained that H.D.'s poem proposes multiple definitions of the spiritual states.

Thirty-five letters between H.D. and Duncan have survived. More were written. H.D.'s letter of 14 July mentions a letter from Duncan written in Spain. Duncan and the painter Jess Collins lived on Mallorca from March 1955 through March 1956. That letter is missing. In the initial letter in the present collection, Duncan writes that "Your letter is so generous," which means that there is a missing letter from Duncan in which he sent a copy of "The Venice Poem"; and that there is another letter from H.D. commenting on the poem. In July 1959 Duncan resumed the correspondence after asking permission to write, which was forwarded by Norman Holmes Pearson to Duncan. The two poets wrote back and forth from that point to August 1961. Duncan claimed (and Robin Blaser confirms) that there was a final letter from H.D., but that document is not among Duncan's papers. Since the relationship with H.D. was so intertwined with the relationship with Norman Holmes Pearson, H.D.'s friend and benefactor, the letter Duncan wrote to him on 28 September 1961, the day H.D. died, has been included as a closing tribute.

Simple errors, like transposed letters and common misspellings, have been corrected silently, but Duncan's abbreviations have been maintained. H.D.'s letters are hand written, except for two, while some of Duncan's are typed and some hand writ-

ten. The configuration of the letters on the page has been preserved. When Duncan wrote fast he used a dash as a period,
which is then followed by a capital beginning a new sentence. I
have inserted periods. Notes have been provided identifying
names and references, as well as identifying matching passages
in H.D. and Duncan's published works.

A Great Admiration

dear H.D.

I am sending you a ms. of some poems written in 1947—*Medieval Scenes* and my New Year poem of this year.[1] I will send you more—your letter was so generous; the joy of someone who may listen to the poem once written is second only to the joy of listening to oneself as one writes. I have publishd none of this; the whole atmosphere of publication now only excites corruptions of competition and ambition in me so profound that they choke off my poet-root. My source is communal and my audience is the audience of friends here who hear everything read; and those, like you, to whom the imagination pays homage. Your answer to the VENICE poem is like a real touch upon a string touchd usually by imaginary fingers.[2] These are my devotions to the language; and to those thru whose spirit it becomes manifest. And who free poetry from its so-long bondage to literature. The arrival of the Sitwells in this country has meant the publication of three beautiful poems in a magazine—*The Quarterly Review of Literature*—especially one called the "Bee-keeper" (I am enclosing it in case you have not yet read it) and in the magazine *Life* photographs of Edith Sitwell in all her splendour; at once magnificent—in one, as even this popular magazine is moved to remark, like a sorceress; and then in another almost childlike.[3] Her fame and, more than that, her inspiration have commanded a new respect. But the Sitwells have not come out here to this coast: so I shall not hear her read, until recordings are available.

Ezra Pound has been for fifteen years now a guiding spirit—I turn still to his work with an increasing love. Two years ago I hitchhiked across the country to see him—and found there, alive and well, just that man whom I had feard to find bigotted or mad. He had been, indeed, I came to learn from Dorothy Pound, when she had arrived a year or so previously, reduced by fear and confusion to a pitiful state. He had been confined—

because he was both judged insane and criminal—to a government ward for the criminally insane, and surrounded by the mad had been permitted only one visitor a week—and then only for fifteen minutes. When I visited him, I found that each day it took all of fifteen minutes for him to begin the conversation, those conversations that went on then for four hours. His life seeming to be in the talk; all the talk of the past; Ford Madox Ford, Wyndham Lewis . . . the host of voices in which he lived. Had I heard his voice long before I met him? Certainly this was the very voice that had stirrd in me when I was sixteen the sense of a community of the dead and the living that was like a stream thru human history.[4] He said that he did not want to write any more on the CANTOS during this time when "his mind was straind"; but he works on a translation of the *Book of Odes* with a sense of appointment.[5] "If I am imprisond for ten years and therefore have a time in which to learn Chinese, I shall be happy." The government now, thru the Library of Congress, arranges that he have everything he wants to work with that is available. Friends have told me that there are times when he becomes excited and insists that if he is given two months to learn Russian he will go to Russia and talk to Stalin and stop the coming war. As he once felt if he could only obtain audience with Mussolini he could stop the last war. No, I have never been to Europe. The life of Venice comes into my imagination from that city in your *Tribute to the Angels;* from the sign of lantern-slides in a course on Medieval architecture (a link thru the magic-lantern itself and thru the day dreams of Venice during the early weeks of the writing of the poem—a link with Proust's Venice-jealousy theme); from the ringing of bells (the Campus here is dominated by a campanile); and from a sentence of Macaulay's quoted in a history lecture during the same period—something like that the Roman Catholic Church and the city of Venice were the two oldest institutions of Europe. There are many other "signs" of Venice. Since the writing of the poem I find myself surrounded by them.—the beautiful ringing of bells in your poem.

4

I am looking forward to *By Avon River.* Early in 1947 I read all of Marlowe—I shall send also the NEW HESPERIDES which I wrote during that period.[6] Shakespeare I read either with trembling or with impatience. *Troilus and Cresside* rec ntly performd here by students. . . . . you must know the profound excitement of the play. Have any poems of yours been printed since the Good Frend which I have copied out from Life and Letters?[7]

dear Mrs Aldington/

Dr. Pearson has forwarded to me your permission to write to you directly in sending *Letters* which was published this year and the typescript of the book which I have just finished "The Field"—well, completed, "given," by my fortieth birthday January 7th of this year.[8] Some time ago I met a young German doctor here who was a Frend of yours and told me that you were working on a poem on the Helen; and who gave me some understanding of the concentration needed in work, as Dr Pearson in turn writes that "she has wanted to be protected so that she could go on with her own writing."[9] I will want then to believe that you will let these books be at hand for the time that seems open for reading them; and that I shall be free to write without imagining that I am pressing you for attentions. The courtesy of writing is that we not be driven to it by a sense of duties, much less that particular bramble of many thorns and few flowers of "keeping up," but open the pages of a book as we will. I was glad to learn thru Dr Pearson that you liked my review of *Selected Poems,* tho I am more aware of what I did not know how to write in that attempt than of the few things that seem right.[10] "Syncretism not euhemerism" once it was allowed so thoroughly prevented me from getting to the meaning I sought. "Not only this but this" opens more than "not this but this"; and then "ism" throws away everything. You will find in *Letters* an owl attendant (no. 27), and just before your "Sagesse" appeard here in *Evergreen Review* with that beautiful visage of the Scops owl, I came across Bulletin 72 of the Smithsonian Institution, *The Owl Sacred Pack of the Fox Indians:*[11]

"Then they began singing. After they had sung he (the Owl) likewise began telling them: 'Well, now I shall tell you about this which we sing. As we sing the manitou hears us. The manitou really hears us. The manitou will not fail to hear us. It is just as if we were singing within the manitous' dwellings. That is why we sing, namely, so the manitous will hear us. They will know when we celebrate a gens festival. And you are to sing loudly when you sing. You shall sing as loud as you can. This is why I tell you. We are not singing sportive songs. It is as if we were weeping, asking for life. You are to think sadly all the time. Do not think of anything unnecessarily during that time. You are only to think quietly when you start singing. And as for this fellow, the drummer, he is to beat the drum vigorously. He is to sing loudly. Do not think of women unnecessarily (during this time). For there is no happy feeling when we die. Our relative feels sadly who sees us no more. That is why I said "quiet" when I told you. It is just as if they, the manitous, will bless us for it. That we should be be mindful of the manitous is why they gave us song. We shall not make them happy; that they have compassion on us; that they bless us is why we are given these songs. Therefore you shall believe me; do as I tell you.

. . . . 'Now I will instruct the women of our gens, this one gens of ours. This truly is how you will think. Do not think, "I am not a man, so that I should listen carefully." You are to remember the songs carefully. You are to listen carefully. And do not think, "if I were a man I would have (share in) the sacred pack." This our grandfather thinks of you exactly as he thinks of us. . . . Do not think of being bashful. You will derive life from it if you do what I tell. You will make these men willing if you do that, that is, if you hum. . . . For life is what we who are mortals think hard,' he said to the women."

I must wait with "The Field" until I have the postage to send it; but *Letters* I am sending by regular mail this week. If you could make provision thru Dr. Pearson for me to see any of your new work in typescript I would be most eager. Yr. recent poems in *Poetry* where the hours appear encourage me who have still to learn the stars in the changes of the sky-year[12]

with continued devotion Robert Duncan

July 14, [1959]

Dear Robert Duncan,

Thank you so much for the Owl sequence—and your offer of the books, which I have time to read now. I have written Norman Pearson that I will try to find some old typescript for you—but that must wait. Have you the poems, the *War Trilogy, The Walls do not fall, Tribute to the Angels* & *The Flowering of the Rod?* I don't know if I have extra copies left. Did you see the "Tribute to Freud"? I could get N.P. to send you that from New Haven. I must re-read the review in *Poetry.* I was deeply touched. What & where is Stinson Beach? I hope I copied it correctly from your envelope. Yes, Erich Heydt told me of meeting you. He may be over again this summer with his Dori. I never answered your letter from Spain—was it? I was deeply involved with some prose, reminiscences of War II in London, that had to be done. I didn't want to talk about it.[13] Well, thank you & I will write again—with all best wishes

from

H.D.

Dear H.D.

Stinson Beach is just north of San Francisco, facing almost south
on the Pacific (so that only during winter months do we have the
sun setting over the ocean). The town is isolated by Tamalpais
which was the mountain of the Tamals, a tribe of Coast Indians
(but also inland at Yosemite, which means the Murderers)—
Tamalpais now being our version of a sanctuary a State Park, to
preserve trees, deer (who are already, in a dry year, invading our
village) and the coast towns from the ravages of "development."

I think I have most of your books. Your imagist poems were
a beginning point, given, in High School.[14] Then years later,
as *The Walls Do Not Fall* began to appear in *Life and Letters ToDay*,
I read and gradually found for my own use whatever of yours I
could.[15] The War Trilogy made it possible, gave a link in a tradition, for me to follow lines of my inheritance within the main
body of a given poetics. *Tribute to Freud* I found too in *Life &*
Letters,[16] and *By Avon River*. What I hope is that *Letters* and "The
Field" contain the homage—but I suspect too that rightly we
take leave of our poems just where that "our"ness changes its
meaning, goes on without us, a shape, and the poet who may be
awakened in reading begins. I am barely now at the point where
my work is beginning to be read, taken as an old thread in some
new weaving "out of the whole cloth," and where I can see how
little the thread's being taken or rejected means. Or rather, how
little I understand or care (can care) for the new use.

But you are most generous and immediate in your note. Do
not hold yourself to respond, it is least what I want. Your atten-
tion in not responding when there is no time is what gives me
permission to correspond.

If Erich Heydt and his Dori do come as far as San Francisco,
may I extend thru you a welcome, and that they might visit.

We discoverd recently that the name of the house we have
here is ELFMERE. Which delighted, for part of our life is just
beyond reach in the fairy lore and another sea /

Robert Duncan

Dear Robert Duncan,

I must thank you for the two envelopes—the typescript & the
book. At once, I found *H.D.* and was happy—more happy, when
I turned to the minute, symbolic *Owl* & the poem. I am finding
out from Norman Pearson if there is an extra copy of "Vale Ave"
that I could send you, typescript. Several of the poems have
been published, the "Vale," the farewell, is followed by the
"Ave," the hail of re-discovery, after the parting, or of Birth
after Death. The sequence is 74 short (or not very long) poems,
written two years ago, when I was so deeply frustrated with
my broken bone—but that is healing & I can get about more,
& even plan a possible trip to USA again. I can't say that I "remember" the re-birth sequence of "Vale," but I lived it & live it.
The lines are conventional—no experiment, a re-living.

This is really just to acknowledge the poems, before I get lost
in them, to thank you—with all blessings from

H.D.

Dear Mrs. Aldington,

Enclosed a copy of "The Field"; the book will eventually have, like *Letters*, a preface— and maybe there told that there is an actual field I returnd to in childhood dreams—but there was no Queen under that hill, only the dancers of my own age, and the wind and the grass.[17] So that years ago when I first found *Leaves of Grass* I always expected to find out, if I were attentive and persistent, what the grass was. But there were, were it there, many daily fields, and my sister and I had secret ways and games —tunnels and caves in the grass. I don't remember what they were. In the Zohar the rabbis agree we have to account for our days, and reading recently about Yoga I found that Bodhisatvas know all their births. Well, and Isis too re-members her Osiris. But I will never get there by memory: I cannot even recite. That sorting of seeds that Psyche was put to (and likewise all enchanted protagonists in Fairy Tales) is such a task.

Let only curiosity and appetite lead you in reading. I would like this to have the full grace of a book—that it be ready for the reader's volition and that it have a life of its own.

Robert Duncan

Dear H.D.

I think of the line in an open form as "propositional" or
"proportional" rather than experimental (tho, it is true, in many
poems in *Letters* I did think of the line as demonstrating what
could be done: but even there, the showing that might have been
a "showing off," an I-can-do-this was concieved as a showing
forth not of an ability in the poet but of a power—and hence
toward a form—in the language. Yes, I agree that your line is
conventional, no experiment, "a re-living" you write. Just as
the line thot of as a showing forth of the form it belongs to (the
poem always in each part projected) verges upon a showing off
of the poet if he usurps the power; so there's a double play in daily
speech where convention can mean the meeting place where we
had as poets in a form that verges upon the conventionality we
rightly distrust where the poet claims the place without the
communion. But there's an experiment, isn't there? in both processes—in that we don't *know?* You have reference thruout your
work to initiatory processes—graduations: well, Freudian analy-
sis is such a school in the modern world. There is a Master in
your Professor Freud as there is a poet in H.D. (as the connec-
tive H.D. / Freud verifies for me my sense of what is happening.
What I want to get across is that I must keep a special perspec-
tive for the poet to thrive, for Robert Duncan is a creature of
ambiance (as I must be warnd again and again in dreams against
laying claim, foreshortend from ambition displays of ordinary
dream powers like flying or evocation) and I've to hold some
Simon Magus in myself back to the ground.[18] And early took the
resolve to obey not to strive, so that whatever virtues there are
in my work are imaginary. Now I have come to realize that all
virtues are honey of that hive. A broken hip-bone, whatever
frustration—the beauty of growing old itself (as now at forty I
begin to learn from the backbone again or rather from the mus-
culature more than from my senses) may be our good share in

the more lashing twisting of a limb for lameness that the hero must have—a safeguard, a good reminder.

My grandmother (of my adoption, for my mother died when I was born, and I was adopted at six months) was an elder in the Hermetic brotherhood—she was what she calld herself "a student" and did learn what she could of astronomy and of plants. For me as a child there was the beneficial sense of the cosmos, of *life* being shared with everything in the universe. But there was the malevolent practice of will-power too; the doctrines of karma and reincarnation were fed to that ambient me so that I must return to the ground always. But fairy tales and mythologies were closer to me than those adult conversations that went on endlessly "over our heads" about astral powers and Atlantean migrations. The "magic" of a story was contained, like the lights in an opal; it was not something one could learn from it or get out of it—but find it always. It "happend," and that for me was the beginning of the true. I could participate in it, loose myself in reading (or in dreaming) as later in writing, but I could not *be* it. Well, there's the longing then to lose myself in life (a great jewel).

To show forth, but it could be showing off if something or someone laid claim to the reality in himself; to communicate, but if it were not a sharing it could be the gnosis of know-all—the American craving to be *in the know;* and then poetry, making— that hoverd on the verge of something made-up. Is that true? The older ones would ask, or is it something you just made up?

The earliest joy in your work was in its evocation of those beings of the Greek world in the here and now. But as *The Walls Do Not Fall* appeared in *Life & Letters* I found a story in which the magic was containd—the magic that must have hoverd behind the fantastic beliefs of my family. There was a conversation between the field of the poems and the field of the life: "An incident here and there" your poem began. So: no experiment, but a conformity—I began in Medieval Scenes to read life. And for all my boldness in declaring, as I have at times, that I have never been baptized, graduated or initiated, that I have no degrees—I am to some degree involved.[19] Now I find, after some six years of weaving that *oeuvre de fantôme* in *Letters* and "The Field" with all its figures of a magical ground, that the *oeuvre de vivant* demands its balance. My hand is dumb in the actual ground. I've got to go all the way round home from the *hérisson* to the hedgehog.[20]

Let me take your blessings and plant them among the garden pinks.

Dear Robert Duncan,

All that you write is most fascinating. And tell me more of
Elfmere & "our life." I hear from Norman Pearson that "The
Field" has been accepted by Macmillan. I am so glad. I agree
with Pearson that you have "the real drive of a poet." I have
marked many passages for re-reading, but if I go into that now,
this letter won't get off till much later. I just wanted to say that
I had "Sagesse" sent to you yesterday. It is the X poems, I think
you saw, on through XXVI. I would be glad if you would "house"
these two sets of poems for me, for the moment. I don't think
Norman Pearson will want them now, as he has copies, but he
may later want an extra copy to send out. It is wonderful to read
such words as "Hermetic brotherhood" and "some Simon Magus
in myself"—one seldom writes or speaks & perhaps the inner
experience, the "magic," as you call it, *had* to be expressed—you
will see in "Vale Ave" & in "Sagesse." Don't hurry to read or
worry to write, in detail. The drawings in *Letters* are delightful,
the format, the binding, the end papers. The "excitement" of
preface II. "Cantos—voices of guides," IV "He finds all our poor
writing as we knew it to be: the Writing" V In particular, Letter
I ("how to brew another cup—") And (more of all this later)
"The Thundermakers," "The old man at Pisa—" "R" roses—
& other roses.[21]

Ever

H.D.

September 3, 1959

Dear H.D.

Erich Heydt and his wife visited Monday afternoon, two days
ago. He was, I think, upset by my being bearded. Why? he asked,
and that was much of the conversation. "To be a man"—but it
was also an acceptance or a reminder of my being forty, *nel
mezzo del carmin di nostra vita* would mean I would be eighty
years.[22] "The most difficult thing about a beard," I told him,
"is that in America it also means nonconformity." So: in part it
means, outside of home or the village here or circles of friends
in the City, being mistaken—and tho it means one is mistaken
for another, it means in part, well, just the part we have in being
mistaken (in dreams, not to know the cues, the lines or the play;
standing unprepared, on stage.) But reading *Letters* and then
The Field you will find another bearded man, whom I also
remember in returning to, accepting, the given beard. "The
natural man" I said to Eric, talking perhaps too fast (so many
who-He-Is were crowding in to answer)—for Erich had to trans-
late for Dori. "Natural" already seemd wrong—and it was important that he was animal. He was a beast. Jess grew a beard
first. He had been reading a biography of George MacDonald
(do you know his *Lilith*)—in the early decades of the 19th century too a beard was mistrusted.[23] For MacDonald, the beard
filld out the image God had given. The religion of Jesus Christ
was intended to restore our natural condition.
    There was the nineteenth centry then. For me, there was first
the promise and romance that attended childhood—the dreams
and quarrels and controversies, as well as laws that had their origin in the Brotherhood; that surrounded my sister and me with
the information that everything was *alive* and that there were elements we did not see or might at times have seen. Presences of
wind and stream, of plant and fire; that all times, or many times,
were present too. As I have written you, your work opend a way

16

back, the bridge (tho there were other bridges, in *The Cantos*, in Yeats, in Joyce and Eliot) to earliest teaching.

But in order to find the Art, or in the nature of American folk-ways, and for my own soul — I turned away from the aesthetic of my family. My father, who died when I was sixteen, had been an architect — a successful one, not a creative one; his allegiance which remaind — tho kept out of his work — was pre-Raphaelite in ambience: but Ruskin in particular. It was the Modern that I found at sixteen — that still appears as a generation of Masters: Stravinsky and Schönberg gave me my scale in which what had been grades appeard as notes, ascending or descending, for the sake of the music. (And now Webern's late contatas appear as epiphanies of the mode); but I remember most clearly the aura "And then went down to the ships, set keel to the breakers, forth on the godly sea," had. I was seventeen, away at college then — a girl whose poetry had impressed me so that I sought her out gave me the instruction: "Stay away from Eliot, you tend to dramatize as it is," and then turning to her Frend "Eliot's too purple. He should read Pound."[24] I went to the bookstore and read those opening lines, just the two, from which dreams of everything poetry could be to fulfill old promises seemd to flow. And returnd again several times, for the same two lines before at last I had the money to buy the volume of XXX Cantos.

I did not mean to go on about the Modern. It remains the nearest crown of many jewels. But I wanted to bring forward or tell you how the thread came forward so that the nineteenth century appeard as the hidden area, the one unknown. In *Selected Poems* you address William Morris. "The Modern" which was once the new was now the old, linked or showd its links (roots and branches) to the larger crown, or a larger figure in the weaving, than was imagined. Rimbaud and Lewis Carroll, MacDonald and Nietzsche. . . . gave new delineations. And there, among the many delineations was the beard. Once acknowledged, I'd to draw my likeness with beard.

Today "Vale Ave" arrived. "Don't hurry to read," you wrote. Both Jess and I read it during the morning for the immediate delight—the narrative carries one along directly enough. Here and there to recognize particular flashings of your signature; and here and there to recognize what must indeed be true. True to the story, and then true somewhere everywhere. Hier & Da shows the actual signature. You have subscribed to it, given it regency. (And here, we found a sawhorse with the signet HD carvd in the crossbar.) I have housed the typescript in a clip-binder with heavy end-boards. With a special joy that surrounds works of the art for me—perhaps that was what I was trying to tell you in telling about first opening Pound's *Cantos*.
In love's name, as he attends our art,

Robert Duncan

Sept. 16 [1959]

Dear R.D.,

Erich has brought news—& tells me of Dori's reactions, too, to the beard. Even Norman Pearson writes, "it was obviously a great point of interest & concern." I have your long letter & the little volume of poems & the birthday poem.[25] I want to be absorbed into them & the other books again, "you will find another bearded man." I don't know the MacDonald *Lilith*, but thank you so much for keeping my MSS, for the moment. If they are in the way, Pearson will take them off your hands. It is interesting about the *Cantos*. Did you see Ezra at St. Liz, as he calls it? I hear very occassionally from Rapallo. The Wm Morris legend meant much to me & it was Ezra who first read me his poems. I am interested in your family story, too & Erich was, "*did he tell you all this?*" I think there are only 4 letters—no, 5, one letter was enclosed with book, but you have told me a great deal. Have you written your story? Alas, I did a great deal during the years in Blitz-London & now am restoring or reviving a re-living this family story for my brother to take back, if he stops at Z[urich]. on his way to boat.[26] He is 72 in Oct. & about the only person in the world who remembers our first home—if he does remember. This is why I can't write as fully as I would—& Pearson also wants me to go over another story that *Grove* may do in in the spring. I will write again. You & Jess & your friends were with us in our two short visits—less than an hour—Erich has his analysands—Dori is even more burdened. But they love their work—& are, in different ways, perceptive & understanding. I am so very happy that you met. They loved your house & the cats.

Thank you again—& I will write more fully, when I crawl out from under my own old MSS.

———

H.D.

November 1, 1959

Dear H.D.

    With the section on my mother the enclosed suite is complete, and I like to think of its having been all there for your birthday, only, I could not quite render it. Let it be a little suite of music, to attend you, not for you to attend.[27]

    Tell Erich and Dori that I shed my beard before going to Portland to read and lecture. I discarded my Adam and went anonymous. Well, I didn't really want to discuss "Why Whiskers."

    Our thots frequently return to you. An editor at Grove writes asking if I would want a thermofax copy of the Coda to "Helen in Egypt". . . and now I must wait for the ripening of these "pointers."[28]

Robert Duncan

Dec. 2 [1959]

Dear Robert Duncan,

I must thank you for the sequence of the Sept. 10 poem—and
now it nears Christmas again. It was kind of you to "house" the
two sets of poems, but now, at your leisure, will you post them
back to Prof. N. H. Pearson, 231 HGS, Yale University New
Haven, Conn.—I enclose check for $30 for "stamps" & perhaps
toward your holiday festivity. I gave your beard or beard-less
message to the Heydts who seemed pleased with your decision,
although they found you delightful as you were last summer.

Forgive inadequate, hurried note. I will try to write again.

With best wishes to you all there & with thanks again for the
Sept. 10 poem.

H.D.

January 2, 1960

Dear H.D.

Texts have a life design of their own. When your letter
came, I was in Seattle where I was reading, and Jess, for I had
askd him to read my mail and as far as I had office to act for me,
obeyd immediately. I might have taken privilege from your "at
your leisure" to copy them and have missd how directly, once
guests in my house, they have left their imprint upon my heart—
where the mind best reads. I have now data on just what remains
most vivid—I had read the "Vale Ave" aloud once, and there I
have my clearest impressions: because I have no text I can be
sure where the words of the song remain, where the feel of the
song lasts—and then there are scenes where the song has agency
for something more vividly seen, heard or felt. What doctrine of
reincarnation can exceed this immediate sharing of loves which
writing opens up for me? Buber in his introduction to *The Tales
of Rabbi Nachiman* refers to a teaching I have not found elsewhere
that a man who is already endowed with a soul can also, in a
certain moment of his life, receive one or more souls that unite
themselves with his own if they are related to it, that is, have
arisen out of the same radiation of the primordial man.[29] The
soul of a dead man joins itself with that of a living man in order
to be able to complete an unfinishd work that it had to leave when
it died. A high, more detached spirit descends in complete fullness of light or in individual rays to an imperfect one to dwell
with him and help him to completion. Or two uncompleted souls
unite in order to supplement and purify each other. If weakness
and helplessness overcome one of these souls, then the other
becomes its mother, bears it in its womb and nourishes it with
its own being.

"Poetry" is a womb of souls, which we as poets attend. In these
poems of yours I at first find data of person, the fable of the actual
"poet" H.D.; then that sense fades before the intensity of the
poem as it unfolds lives, lives—all the persons become persons

of the reader as *me*, and I in turn have gatherd up *having been present where the poem is present*. Thus the Keltic bard bore witness:

> Idno and Heinin calld me Merddin,
> At length every king will call me Taliesin.
> I was with my Lord in the highest sphere.
> On the fall of Lucifer into the depth of hell;
> I have borne a banner before Alexander;[30]

and with the Light fell. But then who is this "I"?

I meant only somehow to say what you know—the light you gave to my house long ago reamins—and the two poems in that light, *Vale Ave* & *Sagesse* were guests that gave benediction,

R.D.

May 13, 1960

Dear H.D.

Norman Pearson suggested I might call this afternoon late to see when I can meet you. I will phone the Stanhope at 3, with that hope.

My reading in Chicago has been set now for the 23rd. There is a party the preceeding day . . . but it does mean I will not have to leave New York until the 20th.

With the exception of the 16th when I read at noon at Brooklyn College, my own time is free. It is there for your service.[31]

Robert Duncan

Dear H.D.

Flying home, covering what had been three days and two
nights by train in four hours by jet, and visually in the range
where mountains are seen as systems—Yosemite valley, a ravine!
the more vast and huge because they are far below (31,000 feet):
I thot of you. That you might make that long (so short) way
across the continent; and of my ancestors too, who—how did
they do it, except there seemd no alternative?— crossd those
barriers of mountain and desert after the Civil War (my grandmother born en route, but already in the Oregon territory; my
grandfather made the trek). Over the land (and over the time too
somehow, going thru time zones so fast that it does not seem
improbable to arrive yesterday), and clear most of the way,
brought me home from New York that with its glass towers, and
its rapidly (since 1956) changing presentation of itself is so fully
1960 with some ghost gatherd from pioneer tales told about the
firelight when I was a child—old folk in the 20s so that the old
trip was made too, from 1864 to come home.

Is it some too wild a hope that you might come to visit? It
could be, if we're to avoid importunities, "without name." Well,
you are very much in my thought, and your part is woven in
with poppies and roses, with the slopes, bronze and green, of
Tamalpais, and the sea. "Flanked by the sea," I wrote to Norman. I am reading "Madrigal,"[32] as if for the first time (I had
read it along the way of train trips and stop-overs). "Wait until
you get back," he had said "and read it"—(at leisure, was it? But
he is a director, right or trustworthy (and with cunning—there
is good cunning, isn't there?) beneficent. It comes true anyway,
the beauty of Madrigal, its returns and correspondences sing
out now (today, just before writing you, writing Norman—the
two voices "The war will never be over" and the "There is no use
trying to believe that all this war really exists. It really doesn't
matter" came thru. For me, now, the novel makes it matter,

25

is a poetry then—what really exists, ποιειν to make it so it is, I take it. And is created for the reader, extending as a part of presence, made memorable.

But I wanted somehow to say C what? of what my visits with you meant. My sense is verified. Does that mean some approximate thing? Am I timorous about intensities? I do not want unnecessary intensities. But your presence had spoken so directly to me in your work, and freed in me some force, even *the* force, of my own work—there *is* a genius, a particular one attending the awakening of what a writing is—and I had that, your acknowledgement and obedience then of the genius—a benediction.

I hope you will see more of Denise Levertov. She is one of my close companions of the way—that in poetry means part-singers of a divided, but in communion united, melody.

And I have written to Norman asking about the typescripts of the three books—the one of the Marshall of the forces of the air; the round table and William Morris's pre-Raphaelite brotherhood; and the Moravian brotherhood.[33] Whether I might have them, one at a time, to read, to extend the ground. And, too, might I type myself a copy for my own use only while they are in my custody. In trust.

With love,

Robert

Dear Robert,

Thank you so much for your long letter. I am very interested
in hearing about the flying home trip. I am fascinated with the
idea, but I can't do it this time. I have an idea, that I will be back
in the fall. I don't want to be unkind, or ungenerous, but, *entre
nous* I have had letters and manuscripts from la M., and then she
rang me up, extravagantly, from California to ask me, to take
care of a manuscript of Ezra Pound.[34] I think, that she thinks,
that I go, or might go to the *Schloss*. Of course I haven't been there,
and felt that it would be to[o] difficult to see Ezra in Kusnacht.
If I come to California in the fall, I really wouldn't want to see
anyone for sometime, but you and your Frend.

I hear from Rosset of Grove, that Hotel Alta Mira Sausalito near
SAN FRANC.[35] is very pleasant and quiet. Do you know this
place? What would you think? I would only want a little apartment. This is just an idea of mine. I would like to have myself
and my MSS all together. I have been enjoying the "Apprehensions" and rereading it, especially "fifth movement"; I love your
"Poppy's and roses" in the letter.[36]

We did see Denise again, and talked of you, and of her Poetry.
I hope to see Norman on Sunday, and will ask him about the
MSS that you speak of.

I have been doing too much, so I have asked Blanche to type this
for me. I will write you later again.

It was really *very good* to see you.

Ever

H.D.

August 10, 1960

Dear H.D.,

I've held your idea of being here, in the practical incognito of
Alta Mira, close to heart. Rosset is quite right that that corner is
both near and removed, it has privacy. Which we would, if you
do come, all do well to add our part to. As I told you in New
York I have by some good chance never met not even know what
la M. looks like. But I have put a distance, that is also a distance
of spirit between myself and the city itself which swarms, as
when I was younger I dreamt of Paris or London swarming,
with the psychic bacteria of "poets." Among whom there are
a few that are dangerous because they have not that valuable
magic that shame is, and live, I take it, in an open disturbance,
fattening upon aversions. The Gnostics had a right intuition
concerning *creation*, in that they sensed it was a complex, and
that, well-what we know as a virus, is twisted in, or twists in
as a vital part. I put "poets" in those quotes to give some such
an uneasy due.

Thoth was scribe of the eternal, most fair, so fair that he
makes whole again. But if he be Hermes too / and Hermes in
turn be mercurial?

I love anyway the revelation that is called magic, but I fear
and abhor its uses. That's my weakness; my strength is that I
would forbear.

Our propitious weather (clear and radiant) is from September
thru November, even into December. Seasons here are odd in
character, you know. Well, its quite in focus that fall be most
radiant; but summer here is more often cold, foggy and when
it is not storming in winter the weather is warm.

The book now for me is the work that goes back to and out
from your writing, so the voice of H.D. is very close. But I let
it lead me out too, cast myself upon impulses, and, because
there were angels, found Ficino's music of the spheres.

Denise Levertov wrote about her reading *Bid Me To Live*—the Madrigal, that is *was* akin. You know that early poem of E.P.'s?

"Aye, I am wistful for my kin of the spirit" it is, your MAD-RIGAL, one of those books thru which, by means of which, I can share something akin: "This is for you," waiting with the all but sure sense "for you to find something I had to tell you." The book led me back to Lawrence's poem "Elysium." The beautiful war poems I already knew.

I am sending a recent poem. *They* arrive and demand their time, where *I* have only to obey.[37]

Robert

Sept. 6 [1960]

Dear Robert,

I just *wasn't* going to write any poetry & then your letter came
& the poem, & Aug. 17, it started me off. Does one *have* to write?
It seems so, from your *Risk*. Mine is a *Risk* too. You have *Ajesha*,
I have another name, but does it too "root. . . at hell gate"? I got
one line from Ezra's last *Thrones*—"so slow is the rose to open."
I become so very impatient with *Thrones*, does not seem to knit
on to the edge of anything. I may be wrong,—but your *Risk* anyway inweaves somewhere.

———

"Lilth, why do they call you a devil,
with Lucifer & Asmodel?
True, the *noms demoniaque* are
donnes sous toutes reserves,
so if I worship Astaroth or Astarte,
I am possibly not yet lost."

———

This is, I suppose, my *Risk*. Does one go on? Rhetorical question! ". . . (she) draws the veil aside,
unbinds my eyes,
commands,
write, write or die."

Cold here—cold & rain. I will write again. This is only to
thank you for writing. I will dream of some *Elysium*.

Ever,

H.D.

Dear H.D.,

"Does one *have* to write?" and "Does one go on" key in with a passage of the writing on the book—I sent you last.[38] Isn't the question the river may ask: péw? In *By Avon River*, in that super-title to the *good frend* and *the quest* there is the suggestion at least of the currents the book finds in history. And I think now, (because I came across a little book by Jessie Weston published by the Quest Society) of how whatever that quest was its earliest text seems to be out of one Bleheris out of Wales, or Blihis, or Bréri, or Bledhericus: Bledri ap Cadivor, master of the story 1070–1150; who sided with the Normans and was called "Latin-arius," "the Interpreter." And Wolfram referd to one Kiot "the Provençal." Jessie Weston tells us there are no texts later than the first quarter of the thirteenth century. The period for this "legend" or wisdom or romance—the flourishing—is "not more than some fifty years."

Some *materia poetica*, "mother," is exciting and excites us, "compels us," to write—if we are vulnerable to or aware of it (Her) at all: to tell the story. And since it is a real matter, all of us, some company, are included. But you know, we may (poets and others have projected over and over the figure of the bee and the rose), serve the flourishing in some function we hardly notice as we go about our honey. But then, bees too perhaps are impatient. They sting, and watching them at work, it does seem to me they almost wriggle with "impatience" or some thing like it.

The bee and the rose—the bee-dance, the sky map and the food-source—is one figure of the command. And let the bee-dance and the sky-map give hint of what we too are calld to to be poets (with some sure instinct that the line must be sweet and also rough, must flow and yet be cut as if in stone) the signatures and the way; the hive, the poem was only home. In the rose we'll read "Elysium."[39]

But I had another figure first on my mind, a river. What "the modern" out-lawed—rhetoric. Fluency. The figure has come from the conjunction in your letter of "Rhetorical question!" and the command "write, write or die!" I saw recently a book of photographs relating life-movements in tree, river, wind-currents: two phases there. How the river too involves and pro-longs (fed by many streams of life) its life in its delta, forming islands, increasing the directions of its way into a network (so, life appears in the networks of a palm or the complexities of the star-map); the other, that the river flows into the sea for miles before its waters are lost to the salt waters, carving its deep channel and raising its shoals.

The river has just its course; then, the Grail romance running its course. Jessie Weston argues versus the Christian theory of origin and the folk-lore theory of origin, for a ritual theory,

The tradition has become hopelessly confused and intri-cate, but it appears to point to an earlier stage at which each manifestation of the Grail was under the charge of an appro-priate Guardian. In the esoteric interpretation this Guardian would represent the Life-Principle, and whereas the Maimed King would correspond closely with the Dead, or Wounded, God, and in this character be present at the general ritual feast, the Fisher King, representing that personage in his full activity, would have charge of the spiritual Vessel, the 'Holy' Grail. The King of the Chastel Mortel, which term can hardly connote other than the Body, the Flesh, would be Keeper of the Grail in its lowest form; and that this was indeed his *rôle* is indicated by the fact that, in the one text in which this character has been preserved, the *Perlesvaus*, he is making war upon the Fisher King for possession of the Lance and the Grail—his own symbols which have here become Christianized and removed from his keeping.[40]

32

for a "tradition"—but the tradition has been created in just these texts that seem to refer to it in such a fragmentary manner. The river is a current of impulses "hopelessly confused and intricate" —so the statistical physicist tells us, but it appears to point towards any one of its springs at an earlier stage. And at last, terminates, lost in the sea—we find no more "Grail" character.

Jessie Weston argues that the Church in its war on heresey had "discouraged" the writing of Grail romances. But an imagination too runs its course, has its life-form.

Traditions are river-beds or species. It's the something unruly of the actual river that compels us to write towards its own ends.

"There was once a river here," or the idea too of underground rivers, that somewhere appear: and up for a time the Grail romance flows thru the lives of those members of the Quest Society: Waite, Jessie Weston, Charles Williams all devotées, Knights asking and answering their question—and then the figure carrying over into Eliot's *The Waste Land*, arousing questions and answers in its readers.

As the powers inherent in the Names and hours I find had the devotion of Ficino (who was devoted too to the Scale of scales), that flows full in your work. And will not, I believe, let us be. All names in Ficino's imagination, in his "tune," were daemonic and possibly devilish; in his sight, they were good.

I've to return to work—your letter has, as you see, set me off to water finding.

Look around in October and see if there is not a time to visit here. The Alta Mira, as I wrote you, does have seclusion.

Robert

Dear H.D.,

I regret in a way sending off the beginning of that chapter to you, for I've had to clear out so much, especially all that attempt at "Chamber" and "music," to work toward reseeing the scene in another light that opens up the way for me, a more fair vista.[41] What I've done is to keep the direction towards the scene on the lawn, and it's, the new thread, all there in "Something once acted had become most real."

I've had a growing sense of what the play means thruout your work. Only this last week I realized that there is such a direct play between Goethe's Helen and yours.

When I have this opening complete now I will send it to you; but I wanted too to write as soon as I could to send you a new poem (tho the first section to come of the poem—part II—is several months old), remembering your speaking of Lang's Fairy Tale books.[42] I've tried in these songs to let the memory of the fairy tales sing.

Robert

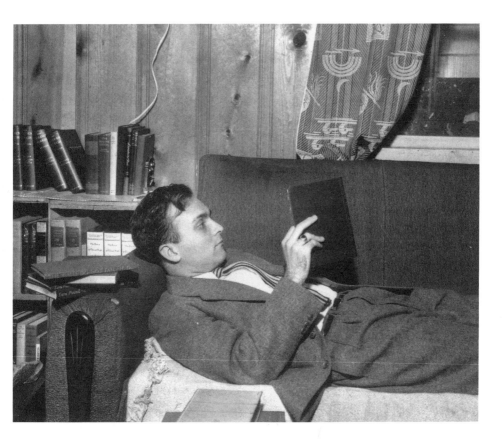

Robert Duncan, Stinson Beach, 1960. A copy of this photo was sent to H.D.

Robert Duncan, 1960. Photo by John C. Ward

Jess, Stinson Beach, 1960. Photo by Harry Jacobus

H.D. at Yale University, 1960

Sept. 28 [1960]

Dear Robert,

I must thank you for your Sept. 22 letter and the reminder of the Andrew Lang books—especially, the *Beast* motive. I have been reading an amazing book, "Yeats's Iconography" in which the author F. A. C. Wilson speaks of bird & beast transformations, among other of Yeats's occult beliefs or symbolism.[43] And I sent you "The Poetry of Ezra Pound, the Pre-Imagist Stage" by N. Christoph de Nagy.[44] I already had a copy of the book, sent me by Norman Pearson—it is the most rewarding critique of E. P. I have read, as deNagy begins *at the beginning*. I don't know if you could do a note or notice of this book anywhere. I know Norman would be glad—& I, also. Now, I have not yet thanked you for the "Study." It is fascinating. When you send the "opening complete" do you want me to return the first copy? I will re-read it, in any case & am deeply touched by the "high-school room." By the way, did you see Ezra in Washington? I would like to know your impression, as I myself finally satisfied myself, as to an E. P. sort of memoir—not to be printed—but I will try later to have fresh copies typed & *possibly* circulate a little. I had a charming letter & some poems from Denise & will hope soon to write her.

This with tardy thanks & all best wishes for the "Study"

H.D.

35

Oct. 1, 1960

Dear H.D.

The de Nagy book on Pound's early work arrived in this
morning's mail along with your letter. You mention Wilson's
book on Yeats; and I am sending you today a book by Virginia
Moore that goes into Yeats's occult tradition more bravely than
others do; printing some passages from Notebooks that other
studies have not touchd (the "spiritual remarriage" of 1909,
pp. 197–204).[45]

I am also sending you copy on the "Study"—but don't return
what I sent you. Destroy it—I have copy of it; but I so regret
where I go astray in it. At the same time I am wary of what goes
on in straying—I've got (like E. P.) a polemic kakadaemon as well
as a endaemon: and so far, the rancor is likely to start its chatter
in the midst of the discourse.

Yes, I visited Pound in 1948 and had two days in Washington,
staying in Dorothy Pound's little apartment and going in the
afternoon to St. Liz's.[46] I had corresponded with him during the
year previous; and in my letters, at the start, made clear my
reverence it was also, *is* a love of the man, for not only had his
work everywhere been a central part of my learning but his
spirit had endeard itself to me—but also my politics which was,
in the tradition of Emerson and Thoreau, and then near too to
the spirit I read in Vanzetti's letters, anarchist where Pound was
so committed to the cause of Fascism.[47] It seemd to me that I saw
in Pound the artist's wanting to have the state a work of art, as
Plato had once wanted a philosopher's state. I was not, anyway,
that trusting of order and coercion, whether political or that
other inner political coercion that Freud saw in the superego.

On pages 7–8 of "Beginnings" you will find some more reflections
on Pound. What was he like in those visits? He was authenti-
cally that man who had been there, thru whom that genius
could come where it does. A manic abundance, excitability,

36

eager to win my ear (the which ear had, after all, come all the way across a continent, hitchhiking, to be in his presence) and even to charm. He put on a little show, deliverd instructions (but they were by rote what was already in his instructive writings).

I had one question to ask him. Had he ever considered the duplicity of powers, words? I had read of a Black Apollo. And then in our own language—what of puns? Didn't everything hint at an ambivalence?

I may have got that far. I had in mind that Pound had been tricked following his righteousness (like Pentheus) into the heart of his wrath, or the political image of his wrath in Fascism, which also was righteous and had its violence.

Pound barked abruptly—and gestured thumbs up! thumbs down! "They pointed which way they meant." A gesture had been lost. Now I would see those dadophori, *Cauti* and *Cautopati*, the light streaming up or the light streaming down, that attend the bull-slaying Mithra.

Pound is at this level or in this person very much *either, or.*

Yet he is not only *either, or* but also the poet of that "godly sea," of the So-shu, churning genius.

At the time I visited, a newspaper in New York had attacked Pound, and a number of writers, "fellow travelers" in large had askd for his conviction and even death. Pound did not refer to it at all, but Dorothy Pound's thought returnd frequently to the conspiracy she felt against him. There was the return of the projected: the man who had the notoriety of anti-semitism would find an actual conspiracy of semitism against him.

The very obstruction, the contention, within the spirit of Pound seems to me an act of the mystery Poetry, the act shows forth under its own orders. Cantos like 90 or 91 in the Rock Drills
Light *compenetrans* of the spirits
Where an Aphrodite that is a creptallive light,[48] a cluster of refractions appears I take as heritage unmixed.

And in *Thrones* these are gists:
"The Temple (hieron) is not for sale"
Getting the feel of it, of his soul. . . .
where the rime shows the mind has been brought into melody—
and

        "Food is the root.
           Feed the people."

How odd that a man shld start about from an M. A., all his life
an instructor, or professor manqué (as Dante was an ambassador
manqué), and come into the genius of Poetry, into the lore of
the Making. It did occur to me that I would believe too readily
that the divine might keep company with publicans and whores,
but find it hard to believe the divine could keep company with
professors and Pharisees.[49]

The professor shows up more and more. He wants to fraternize
with his students and tries slang in his discourse: "grand-dad"—
"gramp," "bumbd off," "fussed about hair-cuts," "that louse G
burnt the Palatine
       and messed up the music
       to speak clearly
απληστια, insatiate κακουργια
This is not a mere stunt to lay fines
       as is found in hodge-podge.

There is in the Cantos themselves, in the poetics of Pound, a
fussing about haircuts that must be included, a messing up the
music, a hodge-podge. May there be a hint of a magic in this
stew. Before the word was in cookery, the O.E.D. tells us: *it may
have had reference to the shaking of things together in a pot of other
than culinary purposes.* (I went to look in the O.E.D. becuase I
suspected a fairy or sprite in Hodge; the nearest was *Hodge-poker*
who was a devil or hob-goblin).

I think I see now what I am after here. We follow the melody
usually as poets, discovering what rimes, along an organization

of feeling that is counterpart of the musician's melodic sense. But there is an urgency (is the [   ] not only a pun here but an etymology) in the genius of our time to break up the mode itself, dissolving there discords the old scale and trying to set once disparate elements into a new harmonia. Pound's recalcitrant off-notes then—if we think of this greater scale of all things toward which we are set to work—is not only a personal insistence but also a demonstration of the genius.

You askd in your last letter your "Why do we write?" but the question you then noted was rhetorical. But *why*, the what is happening in Pound's work, is as much the difficulty as the ease it presents.

Well, the morning has gone away as I wrote. Is there something here that you wanted to hear? The memory of what the man was actually like is pleasing to me. But it is the poet that I have ever on my mind: puzzle over, for much yields no meaning to me; and read aloud in a sapphire, for much evokes the real for me. Yet I must, too, have had some dissatisfaction in the man or he in me, for over the subsequent years correspondence dropped off. By 1950 or 1951, I no longer heard from him—this is the period too, though, of Pound's revived political interests and his gathering about him a group of disciples. I was not sympathetic with that bundle of sticks tied to stand together, the faces: whether it be literary or political. I didn't see things that way. That may have been some of the separation.

In 1955 for his birthday I was asked to write a piece in the Pound newsletter.[50] I started an essay at suggesting the hidden tradition in Pound and was not able to complete it. In 1958 I wrote "The Question" (the "gold" poem in *The Opening of the Field*) as a birthday gift for him; but I never received any acknowledgement. I was perhaps non grata.

Robert

post script: Oct 12. I'd let this sit pending my decision about what I'd done to date on "Beginnings"—and, since, finally, I don't know; I'm sending what is there. Up to part 3, I see how it is going. But part 3 is somehow needed, but perhaps crossed too with threads that I won't finally find in the workings of this study. There should either be more or less of the dis-covery of the patterns of self in it.

Meanwhile, my actual study—reading and working thru *Collected Poems, Palimpsest* and *Red Roses* is opening up for me.

Oct. 18 [1960]

Dear Robert,

It is difficult to write, as I would like to re-read the script &
the letter. You have "assembled" the Ezras. I don't know if you
would care to see a rather *informal* set of notes I did, as he was
about to emerge from St. Liz. Anyway Norman has extra copy
& I will write & ask him—the "notes" are, of course, "personal
and confidential" but it helped me to do them & E. seemed
pleased. I have not heard for a long time. His daughter writes
me that he is not happy at all. I would like to get to Lugano or
Venice to meet them (this is also "confidential") about Xmas, but
there will be difficulties put in my way. I especially like your
portraits of the two girls in the "Study" but I shiver at the thought
of you reading the old prose & poems. To use Yeats's phrase, I am
"dreaming back" but the intermediate writing now seems an obstruction. Of course, it was a way of life, of living. Don't take it
too seriously—I dare not. I must go on, even finding the latest
prose (the E.P. notes) & some new poems, over-revealing (if I
mean that). I find much to explain my reticence or inhibitions
(or *exhibitions*) in the two Wilson books on Yeats. Thank you for
thinking of the Virginia Moore.

I must send this at once or not at all—to thank you & to say
that I will write again. With ever best wishes for the "Study"
& all the rest.

H.

Oct. 27 [1960]

Dear Robert,

The book is hair-raising, to a degree. Now, do you mind, if I write N[orman]. P[earson]. to post you a new copy, & I keep this? It would take so much time for the new book to reach me, & I feel that I *must have it around*, for a time, even if I don't open it. It tempts me from other things. Of course—what a *tour de force*, that digging out the very "secret" R. C. ceremonial! Odd, I met Yeats & "Georgie," as they first called her, & they invited me to Oxford—but something held me back. I did not know that "Georgie" was a medium or he, what he was.[51] I am glad that I had saved (as it were) my real psychic experience for that War II contact. I am glad that I had been working over the two other Yeats' books—a sort of preparation for this. I am infinitely grateful to you—this so sublimely (yes, sublimely) satisfies my curiosity. I must get this to you at once. If I do *not*, hear to the contrary, I will get Norman to post you a new copy.

Gratefully,

H.D.

Oct. 28, 1960

Dear H.D.,

Marjorie McKee has written me that she is going to Europe—
November 10th—for "the tour" with her mother, but then, in
the Spring perhaps to stay on in Italy and paint.[52] She writes
that she met you again after that day when we found you at
the Metropolitian cafeteria—and might she have your address
to write you and possibly visit when she is in Switzerland?

———

Yes, I can imagine how long ago and besides the wench is
dead those poems from before "the war" must seem. But I want
to picture a time or an act of a drama, and have some detective
work to do. There is one question that comes to mind that I
didn't ask in New York. Did you ever meet Jane Harrison? In
a sense, it is not *essential*, for in my practice it's the spirit, some
impersonal wave that I want to draw.

I am looking forward to your memoir of Pound. I love the
"Writing on the Wall," and now, when faced with what the form
of a prose work might be, my mind is overcrowded, expectant,
without conclusion—I the more admire how simply and directly
you have every subtle interweaving between the actual and the
realized.

Robert

Oct. 31, 1960

Dear H.D.

I meant for you to have the book, and I've already asked a
Frend who has a bookstore to find me another copy—it will be
quite inexpensive that way, for he always arranges for me without profit.

The pattern of your "something held me back" is a life pattern
or being pattern—that I find in the way you rime, in the something that holds the sea and the shore in its enduring rhythmic
work. There is a wonder at work, once one searches out the
ceremonial in Yeats. Your disinterest in 1912 was the disinterest
of a growing thing for possibilities outside its law, its real. And
then, the Rosicrucian brotherhood was a church in a way, Yeats
living close as he does to the thought of the Anima Mundi to
phantoms and figures of the gnosis, seems not to have known
or does not in his work bring us into the consciousness of—the
numinous woodland and shoreland, the events of god outside
the ritual. He did not *create* ritual; his initiations prevented that.
And what you or Lawrence (in his "Ship of Death" and "Blue
Gentian" poems) or Pound in the evocation of the gods—(the
Pisan Cantos especially) bring us as a new generation in poetry
is the sense of presence.[53]

And then, the psychic experience may come—that one that
has to do with other orders—only when at least the soul is in the
marginal realm, for those with a full life span there is childhood
then and "old age"—the transitions
"spirits between headlands
and the further rocks"
we've been taught, by the teachings of the good Freud, to read
as meaning the "head" in "headlands."

Well, but Yeats never worked there. There's a play of human
spirit in which Yeats or you or I must be members of a cast,
meaningfully full-filling a design that depends upon what we
are, but where we do not know all. In the poem, we find once

44

the work is there, the full-filling of its structure shows us more than we knew or felt had the work not been done.

You know I was surrounded in my childhood by the cast of a Hermetic Brotherhood, and—tho there was a great point made that children were not to be "initiated," that only in the fullness of the will should anything be known—we were told how we were adopted (my sister and I) by design of the stars; and we were told that we had past-lives. Dreams were read that way, as memories—but memories that gave no pressure in imaginary realms.

Then, after my grandfather's death, when I was about ten; and finally after my father's death; the rites were gone before I came into any fullness of the will.

But what lasted on into the twenties was an after-math of the vital phase. *The Quest* is a summation but also a separation of the ways.[54] I wonder, but what I wanted to assert was the rightness of what held you back, that prepared you, instinct for life or of life. The headlands are most important; the further rocks are most important.

I'm so glad I was able to "find" Virginia Moore's study for you. Who have found so much for me.

Robert

Nov. 6 [1960]

Dear Robert,

Thank you for 2 letters. Certainly, give Marjorie McKee my address—though I am not actually living in Villa Verena, that address always reaches me. I would love to see her and her mother—she may write, anyway—but my own plans are a little uncertain. I *want* to get away for a time, but it is all emphatically "on the knees of the Gods," or on my own knees rather, which don't get any better in this constant fog and premature winter-cold—it is the *damp* chiefly. No, I never met Jane Harrison— your questions always intrigue me. I have already written Norman Pearson to send you the book. Odd that you should write about the "further modes" as I have been working on an intellectual formula, invoking the temple of Athene Hygiea on the island (headland) of Aegina. And how revealing your recall of "the good Frend" and the *head* in *headlands*. I am always astonished by your "Hermetic" inheritance & feel that you were really inspired in sending me the Yeats' book. It satisfied my curiosity and I feel that I am free for the "headlands." Don't take my Ezra notes too seriously—remember they are informal and "confidential." I see reviews of the Charles Norman book on him.[55] Pearson said he was sending it.

My greetings to M.M. and explain how things are.

Ever

H.[56]

46

Dear H.D.

My mother died at the Winter Solstice—Dec. 21st.[57] Not
grievously but in good will. She'd had a heart attack in October,
and we went down to see her when she recoverd. I was a depen-
dent, literally—and that always means expressively too; yet I
can't locate the loss. There was immediately the residue of some
me in childhood who wanted to keep her as person—and in that
me a child's immediate "coming to grief," "being left behind."
But in my adult years there's always been personally distance
between us of mind, of aesthetic, of actual geography—and the
distance of "death" seems so allied that it is hard to remember
I can not, have not to, write a letter.

I've had no echo of her, my heart (from the Oedipal course)
holds against her. But the night she was dying—it was nine
months since my step-father's death, and I think her death was
a labor of a kind—towards him—I could not sleep until after
three-thirty in the morning and worked on an orphic series
I've started. There was just the conjunction of the section of
the poem that began:

> Quickly, quickly, return to earth,
> return to air,
> earth and water have gatherd me about one fire,
> born of the earth, child of the stars[58]

———

And now we've turned on into the lengthening of the days, and
I return to work—
    My thot is often with you
                                    Robert

Jan. 12 [1961]

Dear Robert,

I haven't written you for a long time now, Jan. 2 letter about
your mother who "died at the winter solstice." Mine went at
spring solstice, in her sleep, but there were all the different
distances that you speak of to catch up to or fill in, through
the years.[59] I remember how Dr. Hanns Sachs in Vienna said,
"it takes at least 10 years to realize the death of a parent."[60] I
know, in a way, what he means now. I was in Territet; it suddenly oddly seemed that the *mountains* were or contained my
mother who had died in New Jersey. Of course, I *knew* this
mountain symbolism, your "return to earth," but I had not
felt it.

It is so dark here. It might be Norway. I couldn't arrange a
winter-trip, but possibly, I may come to N.Y. again in March.
This is an inadequate note to thank you for writing—let me
hear again.

H.

Dear H.D.

—The Pound revelations arrived yesterday from Norman. Your writing has more and more—as, for me, too in "Vale Ave" the wonder of a form that has dissolved the character armatures of "style" and takes on nature, an inner nature. But it's just that the inner nature is not taken on, but takes over, emerges.

I've to go as I can; and, as the essay I just finished for *The Nation* reveals to me, I'm all bound up with style.[61] What a blessing then your work, the *Bid Me To Live* and now, the *End to Torment* are. As if my pleasure—it's my spirit taking such direct pleasure as you make those delicious turns in this work, and life and Erich too, co-operating in the Work, in the Alchemical Opus) dance with you. It's lovely.

And I find a pattern to which my mind returns, dream to some figure of life—in the series on the Freud homage, *The Writing on the Wall*, the Lawrence "letter," and the Pound revelations. Writing, bidding, end: wall, live and torment.

There are two immediate afterthoughts I wanted to share. That while Pound père was Homer; Pound himself is Ezra. His name-spirit, in whose name-sake he is, is Jewish: and drawing the sorts out of the King James version: I find; "he was a scribe"; "he had prepared his heart to seek the law of the Lord, and to do *it*, and to teach in Israel statutes and judgments." And, then, too—that it all has to do with those who had married strange wives. The Book of Ezra closes: "All these had taken strange wives: and *some* of them had wives by whom they had children."[62]

Where echoes at one level reverberate with the disclosures of your little opus. And we see too the especial racism of this Jewish scribe of the law that is Ezra's name-patron.

The other afterthought relates to your relating your own persona in the Achilles and Pound's in Odysseus—lover and alter-ego.

In a series of little talks here on personae, persons and places, genni etc. in your world and Ezra's (what we see if we note that those faces in the Metro station of Ezra's are "an apparition"; or if we go into the idea of the image thru to the Image of Christ or of Cybele that was a stone attended by lions or portals):

I found in Brownings's Sordello, searching for Who was my Sordello and then *your* Sordello:

Ah my Sordello, I this once befriend and speak for you. And then below:

What has Sordello found?
Or can his spirit go the might round
At length, end where our souls begun? as says
Old fable, the two doves were sent two ways
About the world—where in the midst they met
Tho' on a shifting waste of sand, men set
Jove's temple?[63]

O, yes, and about your Vidal, Lupa Clues. Sister Bernetta Quinn seems to have kept Roman Christian boundaries in her open speculations.[64] I know that just here, where you are most aware that cults of the Wolf-Zeus existed you are most obedient to that inner nature that will not leap to what we *know*. But I was sent off to look again in Jane Harrison's *Themis* where she traces the story of Romulus and Remus. Denys of Halicarnassos, she tell us, "a Greek by birth, and one to whom Latin was an acquired language" saw or divined "the substantial identity behind the superficial difference" between "Dodona, her sacred oak, her sacred doves, her human god-king Zeus; Tiora, her tree-pillar, her woodpecker, her human god-king Mars."—There's *too much* that's attractive in the discussion. What I wanted to share was that it's not a dove but a woodpecker that appears in the Romulus-Remus story (the Ezra son of Seraiah—Ezra son of Homer story) but *Picus et lupa* Picus "who spurnd the love of Circe" woodpecker = Rock-Driller?
Then Jane Harrison quotes Plutarch:

"The daemons, Picus and Faunis were in some respects (i.e. appearances) like Satyrs and Panes, but in their skill in spells and their magical potency in matters divine they are said to have gone about Italy practicing the same arts as those who in Greece bore the name of Idaean Dakyls."

and later: "Picus himself, according to the Byzantine syncretizers, knew that he was really Zeus"

and from Suidas quotes: " 'When he had handed over the western part of his kingdom he died at the age of 120, and when he was dying he gave orders that his body should be deposited in the island of Crete, and that there should be an inscription: *Here lies dead the Woodpecker who also is Zeus.*' "

"But it may be that you are of sterner mould and of conquering race, that you are an incoming transigent Achaean;" Jane Harrison continues: "you came down into Thessally"

and there it is!

"building a nest like a magpie" the *Chronicle* said (as it comes in your opus. As your "in my own magpie-nest a manger?" reminds us of the Zeus<—>Christos, in the infant. A market basket. Anyway, there, just ahead, it is—your (page 12, March 12th:) Merkur data mentioning "memories of a Capanius (Kapaneus?)

"you come down into Thessally and find the indigenous Salmoneus or it may be Kapaneus at Thebes making thunder and lightning with his rainbirds and waterpails and torches. What! An earthly king, a mortal man, presume to mock Zeus' thunder! Impious wretch, let him persih, blasted by divine inimitable bolt:

Demens! qui nimbos et no imitabile fulmen
Aere et cornipedum pulsu simularet equorum."[65]

51

The passage on *locus* in American Emerson, Thoreau, etc. is along the line of my thought—this to convey, above, to express the impact. I've typed a copy of *End To Torment* both to bring my second involvement to bear on the letter of the text, and—to be able to return the ms. promptly to Norman's care.

I will have

Dear Robert,

I am sending you my rough type-script of "Hermetic Definition."
It is in 3 parts, part 2 is an effort toward balance, an *escape* from
part 1. It is worked around certain phrases of St. John Perse,
whom I met at the time of the Academy Award.[66] He was very
kind & tactful. But "Grove of Academe," part 2, returns to part
1, "Red Rose & a Beggar," in the final solution part 3, "Star of
Day." If you type this out, you can, if the original is in the way,
send it to Norman P., he collects various stages of my work—but
I don't think it necessary. He has (I just sent him) a clear copy,
but I didn't want it hurried to you & back. The Ezra notes got
stuck with Charles Norman who had the MS a very long time.
Your letter is illuminating—did you know you forgot to finish it?
It ends in the middle of a sentence and no signature; "I will
have" ends the letter. I am sorry you had the trouble of the copy.
Your references, quotations etc. are most revealing. Yes, the
name Ezra too is so important—but from the first, contradictory
—his mother called him *Ray*, his father always named him *Son*—
Ray Sun, & Sun-Ray as it was & should have been—I will write
more when I ponder your findings further. This must go out at
once, to bless & thank you.

Ever yours,

H.D.

Dear H.D.

The "Hermetic Definitions" arrived the 4th, I think it was.
And in my first two readings stirs many things, "definitions"
about the art, from the evidence you give so clearly here. The
troubled "decline" (yours, his) of the first part, and the drawing
(from, into); then the Perse-H.D., cosmic-psychic (or spirit-
psychic) of the second. In the last line of "Star of Day," Jess
noted you had alterd the male figure of day to feminine aurora
of Dawn (where above "the unalterable law").

The blowsy almost ice-cream Belle of Portugal rose that climbs
over our porch, framing views of the sea has been in bloom for
almost a month; and the single pre-Raphelite rose deep-pink of
my "At the window the rose vine" too. But the day your "Definitions" arrived, the deep scarlet rose, the first of the year, had
arrived too in the full bud at the point of the unfolding. And
now as I write has opened into its full glory. "The H.D. rose,"
Jess exclaimd this morning.

Is there something in our undertaking religion or magic that
declines, has begun to decline, the open risk of life? Naming
things in the first place, what we work with, becoming Man that
way, was declining the open nameless field itself? Your *Is remembering chiefly a matter / of twig, leaf, grass, stone?* came with some
burden of pathos of the *Psyche* where, seeking Eros, she is sepa-
rated from the utter cosmic reality; and must ask not twig and
leaf of twig and leaf but ask them to help her, ask for their sign,
for their "what-to-do-now." Won't I, I askd after reading these
"Definitions" have let the psyche go at the last? Thinking of the
suffering (as Dewey calls experience "what we suffer, undergo"),
the experience out of which the poem works its way. And of the
other term of the art itself, that it is painstaking.

Yet I felt too a decline, as if you were at many points about to
decline the taking yourself to task in the line. "Only the day's trail"
is on the brink of Perse's cosmos and eternity. (As a wandering

mind comes to that world; and *does* contrast with the pilgrimage-mind).

Were there, workd into the "Red Roses & a Beggar," elements you were aware of that related to my "Venice Poem," sent to you long ago? but the unfolding of the rose was thematic there—and the "Doge" as Iago, the "knowing" Shakespeare. Yet these are eternal ones of the dream.

My mind did call up a poem of William Carlos Williams's of the *Rose* from his early (1922) *Spring and All* which I send on:

> The rose is obsolete
> but each petal ends in
> an edge, the double facet
> cementing the grooved
> columns of air—The edge
> cuts without cutting
> meets—nothing—renews
> itself in metal or porcelain—
>
> whither? It ends—
>
> But if it ends
> the start is begun
> so that to engage roses
> becomes a geometry—
>
> Sharper, neater, more cutting
> figured in majolica—
> the broken plate
> glazed with a rose
>
> Somewhere the sense
> makes copper roses
> steel roses—

The rose carried weight of love
but love is at an end—of roses

If is at the edge of the
petal that love waits

Crisp, worked to defeat
laboredness—fragile
plucked, moist, half-raised
cold, precise, touching

What

The place between the petal's
edge and the

From the petal's edge a line starts
that being of steel
infinitely fine, infinitely
rigid penetrates
the Milky Way
without contact—lifting
from it—neither hanging
nor pushing—

The fragility of the flower
unbruised
penetrates spaces

April 18,
   Where interruptions must be part of the design of even a letter;
above, midway in copying out the Rose poem, Dr Frieske came
to drive me into the city—and only now, ten days later the time
returns to take up my response again.[67] With something in between that does in form my earlier afterthoughts on the anguish

of the "Hermetic Definition" on the "I am forced to hold my lines in doubt," that needs ask "give me the answer;" and even, elsewhere in "Grove of Academe," must declare

> I did not cheat
> nor fake inspiration—[68]

For that day, where April 7th I suddenly stopd midpassage, I was on my way to have an afternoon with an aunt, my father's sister, who is a member of a little group, out of American "New Thought" currents—where old doctrines of the light mix with theosophy, mental healing with Christian tradition of the Spiritus Sanctus. What focuses in all this is my Aunt Alice's own dynamic good will. A love that dominates, where one's sense for the Art would be to keep alive the interchange between oppositions. But I was troubled by your stirring-up the psyche, or thru the psyche setting into motion the agon (it was, finally, I think that I wanted myself to have some phase that would be "old age," living released from the psyche-drama).

What my aunt said in the course of that afternoon—she was telling me about the Light-self or spirit and the unconscious—was that the agony of the psyche is the transition between the wholeness of unconscious and wholeness of conscious life . . . transition?—but it was actually "between," a space or a time, a state. And then she quoted the Gospel of Thomas (from the new Chenoboskian gnostic finds) in a saying of Jesus: *Pity the body that depends on the soul; pity the soul that depends on the body.*[69]

There is in XVI, XVII of the *Groves* perhaps the core of why the anguish—and it is the "but I am not God," the withholding given voice in the poem. Your query

> he sang, did he, in the sun

articulates the Lilith thing for me, where the "decline" or withholding exclaims "How wonderful to strike my breast and cry

'I have sinned, I have sinned'" and I had thought that *sin* was a binding of real to real, body to soul to spirit, that declared the co-existence of reals and selves. There may be in "faith," holding in faith (as Anselm proposes) an acceptance of what is; and in saying I am part of God; I am of God—the poet says I am of what is—where in the poem, too, inspiration *is;* and, as Freud realized in our making-up or *faking* dreams, even in the "faking" stands must [be] revealed.

In George MacDonald's novel or romance *Lilith*, Eve's daughter Mara works in the world to restore Lilith to the living—what Lilith holds on to is *her* existence.[70] "I will not," she says, "I will be myself and not another"—and even when she is brought to tears, and returns the keeping of Adam, she cannot "let go"— in the book, she says to Eve: "Beautiful Eve, persuade your husband to kill me: to you he will listen! Indeed I would but cannot open my hand."

Behind Lilith—it is Lucifer then?—is the shadow.

"It is the great shadow stirring to depart," he (Adam) went on. "Wretched creature, he has himself within him, and cannot rest."

"Father," Mara has said to Adam of Lilith: "take her in thine arms, and carry her to her couch. There she will open her hand, and die into life."

MacDonald taught the restoration of Lucifer—and when Lilith is brought into the sleep of death she asks "How long will I sleep?' and Adam replies: "You and he will be the last to wake in the morning of the universe."

Your "Hermetic Definitions" give Lilith voice in your person (as "you" in the poem is an invaded or adulterated, a mixed person)

> Now you are born
> and its all over,
> will you leave me alone?

is Lilith; and how left-handed, sinister, not to be trusted then the

  now I draw my nun-grey about me

comes to figure in the close—*nun-grey* was the rime that lead to the last word *Day*, after "the unalterable"—somewhere earlier in the poem you had referrd to your *habit*, and one was aware that mine was a habit, as, too that Nun may have hidden *none* (her "Nothing existence" Adam calls what Lilith holds in her clinched hand, in MacDonald's romance)—

Had you, in altering Day to Dawn, tried to alter the poem's course?

In the "Vale Ave" poem—Lilith (as in MacDonald's *Lilith*) is a member of the cast too. Something happens in these "Hermetic Definitions" that troubles the waters, so that the spirits of the poem contend for place (as if there were a place outside the poem, more real, wherein they would stand). As, too, "I am not God" means there is a place outside God to stand.

But there is no place outside the work for the eternal ones of the work to stand. They have just there (as your, my consciousness in the poem, as presence in the poem) in the line as it goes to exist.

Now I find in a mimeographed "lesson" on the *subconscious*, which my aunt gave me: "He also calls it the 'book' and he said 'We are not any wiser than the book we have written' "—where I would take "we" to mean the poet, as any one of us know or enact him.

[Holograph manuscript of RD's poem "After Reading *Hermetic Definitions*" follows.]

June 28, 1961

Dear H.D.,

Now news comes that you are recovering—I had been fearful and not wanted to send word then, and now hopeful that my writing will be without trouble. Drawing an ideogram from the Tarot for the writing of my book about your work the Goat of Mendes had governed "fears and hopes"—it has been a process of shifty fears and hopes, about the shape and disturbance of the writing itself (the Goat had to do with my own course during the period). There had been too, most gracious, *The Star* as governor.[71]

With the news from Grove came page proofs of *Helen in Egypt*, which I've only just collated for my use, and begun reading, with too much excitement now for reflections and articulated responses. I do see how Claribel opend up for you a key dimension in Helen.[72]

I would send a good wish to attend you. I do not think my wish can perform many services yet, but let him accompany you, a devoted page—no hero, no wise doctor—but dreaming of both. Our thoughts go with you.

Had I written that we too were moving when you were? We're in the city of San Francisco now—with a rather garish accommodating rose in front. But we brought with us—it must be our H.D. rose now that the deep red has been left behind—a wild mountain rose that we all but gave up, for having bloomed the stem dried back. Now a new brightest green shoot has started out, almost two inches in the last three days.

Do not make the effort to answer—for we will hear how you are, and know you think of us fondly. It will make it easier to write, if I am sure you will not feel obliged to *correspond*.

Robert

I cannot find your last letter, so I send this to the Villa Verena, knowing it will be forwarded. For your own records my address now is:

3735 Twentieth Street
San Francisco 10, California

Dear H.D.

My thought and hopes go often to you—in the midst of study
where the life of your imagination and inspiration is constantly
before me; but also, from our few brief meetings in the fond
directive or memories—towards your recovery. For a little over
a month I've been in Vancouver reading again the works of St.
John Perse, for I had been askd to do an article on his work—and
had obeyed the correlation (where your "Hermetic Definitions"
had carried a part of the directive).[73]

But now, the little group that has been attending the unfolding of my "H.D. book" and I have begun the *Helen in Egypt*, and
I find, whatever else there may be, there was preparation for our
reading in what had appeard risky castings out of nets to catch
what fish from the *War Trilogy*.

My own personal reading of the *Helen* came as soon as I received
the page proofs (Norman had askd Grove to send them), and while
I am holding back from knowing, as much as I can—the music
and the weaving of the narrative is immediate. To move as the
soul moves! From the *Walls Do Not Fall* on your work appears as
a total oevure, a communication in interrelations of a universe—
Where *Helen in Egypt* extends and deepens your revelation.

Love
Robert

Sept. 28 / 61

Dear Norman,

Robin Blaser just called, with the news of H. D.'s death.[74]
Upon the very eve of her book—for the first copy arrived on this
coast yesterday. Yet in her aphasia, she was spared that question
broken away from its words that contain the answer, spared the
dumb—no, speechless—effort to grasp the fact.

You will understand how even in my few meetings with her,
she had become most dear. So that in this last period, since her
stroke, my thought has gone back and back to the little vision I've
had thru your correspondence of her in some room, in a garden.
What did it mean to come to what she most feared in herself, to
be at a loss for words? The struggle for saying, I remember, was
pathetic, as if she must reach out to touch the panic of the inex-
pressible. And now that is done. After the dream, the delirium,
the trance—death, the "at last."

It's been a year since the first pages of the H. D. book began,
after months of notes and readings—and my mind has dwelt
upon and worked in reference to that H. D. of the poetry, the
making. She might have liked parts of it. There have been times
when things emerged that I thought would most please her. Yet
I felt thruout too how reticient she was about what touchd upon
her spirit—Would the book be disturbing?

Well, Norman, I can't get at any sufficient thing. I have some
idea of the joy you have in her service. You are, for me, you
know, a Friend in H. D. My study has only deepend my source
there, and now I wish I could console us, or me in you, for the
loss of the possible company. Yet we remain of her company
and there's the parting companions of a way have: "may we meet
again." Wednesday, the day of her death, I was reading in Morris's *Well at the World's End* of the death of the Lady of Abundance.[75] Please, let my words go stumbling as they do here, for I
had to write you, to let my own troubled heart this morning.

63

I send on a poem I began Tuesday of this week,

Love
Robert

DOVES

1.

Mother of mouthings,
the grey doves in your many branches
code and decode what warnings
we call recall of love's watery tones?

hur-r-r-r-r
har-r-r-r-r
hur-r-r-r-r

She raises the bedroom windows
to let in the air and pearl-grey
    light of morning
where the first world stripped of its name extends,
where initial things go
beckoning dove-sounds recur
    taking what we know of them

from the soul leaps to the tongue's tips
    as if to tell
                what secret
in the word for it.

2.

The bird's claws scraping the ledges.
I hear the rustling of wings—is it evening?
the wood-winds chortling or piping,

sounds settling down in the dark pit where the reading lamps glow
as the curtain rises, and in the living room
lamps are lit.

3.

The lady in the shade of the boughs
held a dove in her two hands,
let it fly up from the bowl she made
as if a word had left her lips.

Now that the song has flown
the tree shakes, rustling in the wind
with not stars of its own
for all the nets of words are gone.

The lady holds nothing in her two hands
cupped. The catches of the years are done.
And the wood-light floods and overflows
the bowl she holds like a question.
                              Voices of children
from playgrounds come
sounding on the wind without names
—we cannot tell who they are there
we once were too under what stars?

Before words, after words, hands
lifted as a bowl for water, or prayer.
For what we heard was no more than the dove's

    hu-r-r-r
    ha-r-r-r
    hu-r-r
                    where the day slept
after noon, in the light's blur and shade

the Queen of the Tree's Talking
hears only the leaf sound,
whir-r-r-r of wings in the boughs,
    the voices in the wind verging into leaf sound.

  4.

I wanted to say something,
that my heart had such a burden,
or needed a burden in order to say something.

Take what mask to find words
and as an old man come forward
into a speech he had long waited for,

had on the tip of his tongue this bud
from which now: O fateful thread,
sentence that thru my song most moved,

now from your course the flame has fled
making but words of what I loved.[76]

The most of this (from 2. on) was last night. I was not referring
directly to death but to the loss of words or the return of words
into their initial realm of soundings. Now that the news comes
all the direction seems to speak of death, to my own pictures.
    For her, as for Whitman, and Lawrence, and Pound—there
was the "skiff" or "caravel," the ship of Death, eidólon yacht,
Ra-Set's barge. Very like the little boats that once in nursery
nights carried us out into sleep.

66

Notes

1. The title of RD's poem of 1949, unpublished, is "New Year Poem." *Medieval Scenes* (San Francisco: Centaur Press, 1950).

2. RD's "The Venice Poem" appeared in his *Poems 1948–49* (Berkeley: Berkeley Miscellany Editions, 1949).

3. Edith Sitwell, "The Bee-keeper," *The Quarterly Review of Literature* 4, no. 3 (1948): 232; "The Sitwells: Life Reports Visit to US by Celebrated Literary Teams of Edith and Brother Osbert." *Life*, 6 December 1948, 164ff.

4. RD first read Ezra Pound's *A Draft of XXX Cantos* (New York: Farrar & Rinehart, 1933) in Berkeley, in 1938. See his account in "The H.D. Book, Part II, Chapter 3," *IO*, no. 6 (Summer 1969): 137; and the following letter of RD to H.D. 3 September 1959.

5. The translations were first published as *The Classic Anthology Defined by Confucius* (Cambridge: Harvard University Press, 1954), and then reprinted as *The Confucian Odes: The Classic Anthology Defined by Confucius* (New York: New Directions, 1959).

6. The words from "I shall" to "that period" have been crossed out and replaced at the bottom of the letter with the words "Too laborious a typing job now." "New Hesperides: At Marlowe's Tomb" was written in 1947, but not published until *Manroot*, no. 10 (Fall 1974 / Winter 1975): 28–34.

7. "Good Frend" [Part I, "The Tempest"], *Life and Letters To-Day*, 53 (April 1947): 34–37 and "Good Frend" [Part II, "Rosemary"], *Life and Letters To-Day*, 54 (July 1947): 35–42; collected, with a third part, "Claribel's Way to God," in *By Avon River* (NY: The MacMillan, Co., 1947): 5–25.

8. *The Field* was published as *The Opening of the Field* (New York: Grove Press, 1960).

9. The reference here is to Erich Heydt, who later became H.D.'s principal physician. See the following letters, especially RD to H.D. dated 14 July 1959, and *End to Torment*.

10. "In the Sight of A Lyre, Little Spear, A Chair," *Poetry*, 95, no. 4 (January 1958): 256–260.

11. RD is referring to H.D.'s poem "Sagesse," *Evergreen Review*, no. 5 (Summer 1958): 71–73. RD's poem, "Song what do you see, my little one? I see an owl hung in a tree" is part of "An Owl Is A Only Bird of Poetry," poem xxvii in *Letters*, (Jargon Society: Highlands, N.C., 1958). RD quoted a passages from "The Owl Sacred Pack of the Fox Indians" on a postcard to Charles Olson dated [July 1959].

12. "Regents of the Night," *Poetry*, 94, (no. 2 (May 1959): 71–73.

13. H.D. is no doubt referring to her unpublished journal essay "Compassionate Friendship," written between 18 February and 21 September 1955. RD lived on Mallorca from March 1955 to March 1956.

14. See RD's account of this movement in his work in "The H.D. Book, Part 1, Chapter 1," *Coyote's Journal*, nos. 5/6 (July 1966): 8–31.

15. RD is confusing *The Walls Do Not Fall* with *The Flowering of the Rod*, which appeared in *Life and Letters To-Day* in the following installments: 33 (April 1942): [42]–45; 35 (Oct. 1942): 17–18; 35 (Nov. 1942): 87–88. See also RD's letter to H.D., 15 August 1959 below.

16. *Tribute to Freud* appeared in *Life and Letters To-Day* under the title "Writing on the Wall" in the following installments: 45 (May 1945): 67–98; 46 (June 1945): 137–154; 46 (August 1945): 72–89; 46 (September 1945): 136–151; 48 (January 1946): 33–45.

17. The first poem in *The Opening of the Field*, "Often I Am Permitted to Return to a Meadow," contains the line. "She it is Queen Under The Hill." See RD's account of his dream in "The

H.D.Book, Part 1, Chapter 5," *Stony / Brook* nos. 1 / 2 (Fall 1968): 18–19.

18. Simon Magus, a first century prophet, mentioned in Acts 8:9–24. Supernatural powers were attributed to him. He was considered the incarnation of Zeus, and his companion Helena was considered the incarnation of Athena. He is credited with the founding of the Gnostic heresies within early Christianity.

19. In a essay RD wrote: "I have written elsewhere that I am unbaptized, uninitiated, ungraduated, unanalyzed. I had in mind that my worship belonged to no church, that my mysteries belonged to no cult, that my learning belonged to no institution, that my imagination of my self belonged to no philosophic system." "The H.D. Book, Part 1, Chapter 2," *The Coyote's Journal*, nos. 5 / 6 (1967): 27.

20. See RD's account in "The H.D. Book, Part 11, Chapter 2," *Caterpillar*, no. 6 (April 1969): 36, 37. See also H.D. *The Hedgehog* (London: Brenden Publishing Co., 1936).

21. *Letters* contains a preface which H.D. quotes here. The preface is numbered "preface i–iv" which makes it appear as if the parts of the preface and not the pages are numbered. "The Thundermakers" and "The old man at Pisa," and "roses" appear in RD's piece "A Poem Beginning With A Line From Pindar" which appeared in *The Opening of the Field*, pp. 63–64.

22. The reference here is to the opening line of Dante's *Divine Comedy*. See also RD's poem "Nel Mezzo del Cammin di Nostra Vita," *National Review*, 10, no. 1 (14 January 1961): 20; collected in *Roots and Branches* (New York: Charles Scribners Sons, 1964): 21–24.

23. Greville MacDonald, *George MacDonald and His Wife* (New York: Dial Press, 1924); George MacDonald, *Lilith* (London: Chatto & Windus, 1895).

24. RD's account of this conversation with Louise Antoinette Krause and Robert Bartlett Haas appears in "The H.D. Book, Part 1, Chapter 2," *Coyote's Journal*, no. 8 (1967): 28.

25. The reference is to a typescript of RD's poem "A Sequence

of Poems for H. D.'s Birthday," which accompanied RD's letter of 3 September 1959. At this date the poem is incomplete. "The little volume of poems" has not been identified.

26. Harold Doolittle (b. 1888).

27. RD's poem "A Sequence of Poems for H. D.'s Birthday," has the subtitle "September 10, 1959." Finished October 24, 1959. H. D. refers to "the Sept. 10 poem" in the following letter.

28. The editor at Grove Press was Jeanie Unger.

29. Martin Buber, *The Tales of Rabbi Nachiman*, tr. Maurice Friedman (New York: Horizon Press, 1956).

30. *The Mabinogion*, tr. Lady Charlotte Guest (New York: Everyman Library, 1906): 273. RD is quoting the poem from this translation.

31. RD met with H. D. 4:00–9:30 P.M. on 13 May 1960; he and Denise Levertov had lunch with H. D. at The Metropolitan Museum on 20 May 1960. See note to letter dated 14 March [1961].

32. Published as *Bid Me to Live (A Madrigal)* (New York: Grove Press, 1960).

33. RD is referring to three unpublished novels by H. D. "The Sword Went Out to Sea," "The White Rose and the Red," and "The Mystery."

34. Sheri Martinelli is an admirer and student of Ezra Pound who appears as Undine in *End to Torment*.

35. Barney Rosset, founder of the original Grove Press. Grove published H. D.'s *Selected Poems* and *Bid Me to Live*.

36. RD sent a ditto master copy of his poem "Apprehensions" to H. D. and inscribed it "for H. D., May 1960, Robert Duncan."

37. The poem is "Risk," collected in RD's *Roots and Branches*, pp. 56–59. H. D. refers to the poem in her letter dated 6 September 1960.

38. This letter was not mailed by RD.

39. See RD's essay "[The Matter of the Bees]," *Caesar's Gate: Poems 1949–50 with Paste-ups by Jess* (Berkeley: Sand Dollar, 1972): 61–71.

40. Jessie Weston, *The Quest for the Holy Grail*. (London: G. Bell, 1913): 5–10, 31–2. This book was published as part of The Quest Series, edited by G.R.S. Mead. The Quest Society was an offshoot of Madame Blavatsky's Theosophical Society. It was founded by G.R.S. Mead who had been Blavatsky's secretary. See RD's account "The H.D. Book, Part 1, Chapter 5," *Stony/Brook*, nos. 1/2 (Fall 1968): 13–16. Later in this letter RD mentions Waite, Charles Williams and Knights. Arthur Edward Waite (1857–1942), the distinguished and prolific scholar on occult matters, but best known for his *The Holy Kabbalah* (New York: The Macmillan Co., 1929), *The Pictorial Key to the Tarot* (1910; rev. ed., London: W. Rider & Son, Ltd, 1920), which is a key to a tarot deck commonly called "the Waite deck." Charles Williams (1886–1945) was a British novelist and theologian. RD had read his novels, *The Greater Trumps* (New York: Pellegrinen & Cudady, 1950), for example, and he praised William's book on Dante, *The Figure of Beatrice* (London: Faber and Faber, 1943). George Wilson Knight (b. 1897) is a distinguished and well published scholar who has written books on Byron and Pope, but he is best known for his books on Shakespeare, especially *The Wheel of Fire: Essays in Interpretation of Shakespeare's Tragedies* (London: Oxford University Press, 1930).

41. This letter was written on a typescript of RD's poem "Four Songs the Night Nurse Sang." The chapter mentioned here refers to a typescript of the the first chapter of "The H.D. Book" which RD mailed to H.D. in early September 1960.

42. Beginning with *The Blue Fairy Book* (1889) and ending with *The Lilac Fairy Book* (1910), Andrew Lang edited and prefaced twelve books of fairy stories each titled with a different color—e.g. yellow, pink, brown, olive.

43. Francis Alexander Charles Cauvin Wilson, *Yeats Iconography*, (London: Gollancz, 1960); and his *W.B. Yeats and Tradition* (London: Gollancz, 1958).

44. N. Christoph de Nagy, *The Poetry of Ezra Pound: The Pre-Imagist Stage* (Bern: A. Francke A G Verlag, 1960).

45. Virginia Moore, *The Unicorns* (New York: Macmillan, 1954).

46. RD visited Pound at St. Elizabeth's on 14 and 15 August 1947.

47. *The Letters of Saco and Vanzetti*, ed. Marion Denman Frankfurt and Gardner Jackson (New York: Viking Press, 1956). RD mentions this book from his private library several times in essays and interviews.

48. RD's version of *crepitating*, crackling.

49. In his piece entitled "Pages from a Notebook," *The Artist's View*, no. 5 (July 1953): [2–4] RD wrote "I am a poet, self-declared, manqué." Charles Olson began his response, "Against Wisdom as Such," *The Black Mountain Review*, 1, no. 1 (Spring 1954): 35–39, with reference to RD's statement.

50. *The Pound Newsletter*, no. 7 (July 1955) had a note attached which invited readers who wanted to "add their voices to this collective celebration are cordially invited to send contributions" for the October issue of the newsletter. RD's essay was not submitted.

51. RD cites the passage from "Of course" to "what he was" in "The H.D. Book, Part II, Chapter 1," *Sumac*, 1, no. 1 (Fall 1968): 112.

52. Margorie McKee (a painter) and RD were married 1943–1945.

53. RD is referring to Lawrence's book *The Ship of Death* (London: Martin Secker, 1933) which contained the poems "The Ship of Death" and "Bavarian Gentians."

54. *The Quest*, ed. G.R.S. Mead appeared in 21 volumes between October 1909 and July 1930.

55. Charles Norman (b. 1904): as a poet the author of several books including *Selected Poems* (New York: Macmillan, 1962); as a scholar author of two books about Ezra Pound, *The Case of Ezra Pound* (New York: The Bodley Head, 1948) and *Ezra Pound* (New York: Macmillan, 1960). The last is a biography of Pound.

56. On 22 November 1960 RD sent H.D. a typescript of his

poem "Osiris and Set." At the beginning of the poem he noted "This morning brought this poem," and at the end "I found Set, as prow of the Boat, in Clark, *Myth & Symbol of Ancient Egypt*." [Robert Thomas Rundle, *Myth and Symbol in Ancient Egypt* (New York: Grove Press, 1959).] This typescript has not been reproduced.

57. RD's adopted mother was Minnehaha Harris Symmes (1887–1960), and his adopted father was Edwin Joseph Symmes (1883–1935).

58. The "orphic series" refers to "A Set of Romantic Hymns," collected in *Roots and Branches*, pp. 106–115. These lines are unidentified.

59. Helen Wolle Doolittle (1853–1927).

60. Dr. Hans Sachs, a follower of Freud, Bryher's psychiatrist.

61. The essay referred to here was published as "Ideas of The Meaning of Form," *Kulchur*, no. 4 (1961): 60–74.

62. Ezra 7:10–11; Ezra 10:44.

63. "Sordello," ll. 603–609.

64. Sister Mary Bernetta Quinn, author *The Metaphoric Tradition in Modern Poetry* (New Brunswick, N.J.: Rutgers University Press, 1955).

65. Jane Harrison, *Themis*. 1927. (Reprint. Cleveland: World Publishers, 1969): 102, 107, 109.

66. H.D. was in New York City in May, 1960 to receive a Gold Medal from The American Academy and Institute of Arts and Letters. She met St John Perse at the ceremony.

67. Dr. Oliver Frieske, an anesthesiologist, who lived at Stinson Beach, and who gave RD rides to and from San Francisco from time to time.

68. "Grove of Academe" is the second part of "Hermetic Definition."

69. See James M. Robinson et al, *The Nag Hammadi Library in English* (San Francisco: Harper & Rowe Publishers, 1977).

70. George MacDonald, *Lilith* (London: Chatto & Windus, 1895).

71. The Star card, XVII of the Major Arcana in the Tarot deck of Arthur Edward Waite, was pinned to a bulletin board above RD's typing desk.

72. Claribel: the reference is to H.D.'s poem "Good Frend." See endnote 7, and RD's account of the poem in "The H.D. Book, Book II, Chapter 6," *The Southern Review*, 21, no. 1 (January 1985): 28.

73. The essay was published as "The Poetic Vocation: St John Perse," *Jubilee: A Magazine of the Church and her People*, 9, no. 7 (November 1961): 36–41.

74. Robin Blaser (b. 1925), poet and close friend of RD who shared the devotion to H.D.'s work. H.D. died in Zurich, Switzerland, 28 September 1961.

75. William Morris, *Well at the World's End* (London: Longmans, Green and Co., 1896).

76. This is a manuscript version of the poem, which was revised and collected in *Roots and Branches*, pp. 86–88.